The Gold Half Sovereign

Michael A. Marsh F.R.N.S.

Michael A. Marsh
Cambridge Coins
18ᴮ Chesterton Road
Cambridge CB4 3AX
England
1982

First Edition 1982

Printed by Heffers Printers Limited
ISBN 0 9506929 1 3

CONTENTS

PREFACE

My first book "The Gold Sovereign" was published by Cambridge Coins in 1980. Since then I have had many requests for a similar book on the half sovereign.

I must confess I have had more than a passing interest in this coin, for after all it is very closely linked to the sovereign, my favourite coin. Most sovereign collectors would, I am sure, think along similar lines since the two coins do really bracket themselves in many ways.

The gold half sovereign is of course a coin in its own right and therefore, I feel, worthy of a place of its own between two covers. I will do my best to tell you as much as possible about the currency half sovereign of Britain.

Collectors who become interested in the half sovereign will have quite a range of varieties to aim at starting with George III, then George IV, William IV, Victoria, Edward VII and finally George V. In all these reigns there are many varieties of the currency half sovereign. Alas none were issued during the reign of George VI or our present Queen Elizabeth II.

Generally speaking the collector will find it easy to acquire quite a few coins in the series as there are many that rate as common. However, like the sovereign series some of these coins will be extremely difficult to find in good condition. I must also say that in general half sovereigns were struck in much smaller quantities than the sovereign, and thus the series contains many rare dates and varieties. I certainly find the series full of interest and fascination.

Now as far as monetary values are concerned, you will note that quite a few are mentioned in the text throughout. This I feel is the best way but bearing in mind how quickly values change these days, it is really pointless listing all. Those I have referred to should however help collectors to give a broad assessment of value to most coins.

To enable a rarity rating to be given, every half sovereign type and variety has been separately listed, numbered and rated, these commencing at 400 to avoid confusion with my numbering of sovereigns. I have used the same type of list for this purpose as the one used in "The Gold Sovereign"; it does seem most adequate, although I must stress again that this list is based on coins being found in very fine condition. When some of the more common coins are found in extremely fine to uncirculated grades, then they become considerably more rare and very much more costly too.

MICHAEL A. MARSH

C   Common
N   Normal (Not scarce or common)
S   Scarce
R   Rare
R2 Very Rare
R3 Extremely Rare
R4 15 to 25 examples known
R5 9 to 14 examples known
R6 4 to 8 examples known
R7 Highest rarity possible

ACKNOWLEDGEMENTS

I must at this stage offer my sincere thanks to those who have kindly assisted me in the compilation of this book. Their help has, I am sure, created a better book.

 To the following I say thank you very much, your efforts were much appreciated.

The Royal Mint
The Royal Australian Mint
H.M. Stationery Office
The British Museum, London
The Fitzwilliam Museum, Cambridge
Mr. Frank Bird (Photographer)
The Cambridge Scanning Co. Ltd.
Mr. E. W. Faver
Mr. M. F. Howard, M.B.E., M.A.
Mr. K. A. Jacob, F.R.N.S.
Mr. H. Mountain
Mr. J. H. Mulholland
Mr. and Mrs. J. F. W. Story
Mr. A. R. Turner

MICHAEL A. MARSH

LIST OF ILLUSTRATIONS

GEORGE III 1760–1820

The half sovereign and the sovereign were the first gold coins to be struck for circulation when the new recoinage of George III took place in 1816.

The half sovereign was first struck bearing the date of 1817, its value was ten shillings and it was introduced to replace the seven shilling piece. Benedetto Pistrucci, that legendary Italian, was the engraver.

Pistrucci is probably best known for the famous design that occupies the reverse of the first sovereign, St. George armed with a broken spear sitting on a horse encountering a dragon. This famous design is however not to be found on the first half sovereign. Its place is taken by a shield which I will fully describe later. Pistrucci's design of the half sovereign was approved and the coin proclaimed legal tender on 10th October 1817. It is worth noting that £4,275,000 of gold coin was issued that year, for the completion of the new coinage. The deputy master of the Mint received the sum of £1000. Pistrucci, who contributed so much to the new gold coinage, was paid fees amounting to £1322 for the year.

Before going further into the dates and varieties of this reign this is an ideal time to write of colons. In the past I feel too many numismatists have been far too inventive in their suggestions relating to colons. The occasions when one can really be sure as to why a colon should be in a particular position, are I am sure not often. The first half sovereign does give an opportunity to describe a colon that has been quite deliberately placed in a slanting position. The colon at the end of the legend on the coin's reverse is shown slanting sharply inwards towards the foot of the letter F. This has been done to avoid its being too close to the bottom of the shield, the point of the shield does in fact encroach into the legend area. A colon placed in the proper upright way would give a very cramped impression in circumstances such as this. I do believe that this is an occasion when a definite reason can be given for a slanting colon.

Currency half sovereigns were issued for the years 1817, 1818 and 1820. None were issued for 1819. A good specimen of either of the first two dates would cost about £500. The collector should not have any difficulty in obtaining a specimen for each of these years, though the 1820 coin might be a little difficult. However, the 1818 over 17 is a far different proposition, it seldom appears, and when it does it will cost a great deal of money, for it is without doubt the most important half sovereign of this reign.

Most numismatists are well aware of the many overdates and error dates that are found amongst the silver and copper coins of England;

1

they are well recorded. However, in the field of modern gold this is not so, they are seldom found: when they are they must be classified as extremely rare. I spent many years of patient searching for this variety in the sovereign series, only recently did my efforts yield success and enable me to record the first overdate from the London mint. When you have read this book you will realise that overdates are generally scarce in this series. Why should this be so? I believe the reason for this is that we are talking of *gold*. This was the precious metal of the day and considered very much so at the Mint, therefore I feel that much more care was being taken when the dies were being made for gold coins. Also, it is very likely that the staff involved would have been the best of those who were employed. Extra care, I am sure, would have been the order of the day when gold was being coined.

As time goes by I am sure we will see that few such varieties are added to a very scant list.

Description and details of the new Half Sovereign

Obverse. The King's head facing right, laureate, hair short; the tye has a loop and two hanging ends; the neck is bare. The legend commencing at the bottom of the coin, GEORGIUS III DEI GRATIA. The date is at the bottom of the coin below the truncation.
Reverse. An angular shield, surmounted by the royal crown, bearing the Ensigns Armorial of the United Kingdom. The Hanoverian arms within an escutcheon surmounted by the royal crown in the centre of the shield. The legend begins at the bottom, it is interrupted by the crown at the top and it reads ·BRITANNIARUM REX FID: DEF· The coin is struck with a reverse die axis.
Edge. Cross graining.
The weight of the new coin was to be 61.637 grains.
The fineness is 22 carat with 11/12 fine gold and 1/12 alloy.
Millesimal fineness 916.66.
The weight and fineness of the half sovereign remain the same throughout the whole series.

HALF SOVEREIGNS OF GEORGE III

NO.	DATE	VARIETIES	MINTAGE	RATING
400	1817		2,080,197	C
401	1818		1,030,286	C
401A	1818/17	Obv. overdate 18 over 17	Not known	R6
402	1820		35,043	S

GEORGE III

Plate 1

Actual size

Obverse of Half Sovereign No. 400.

Reverse of Half Sovereign No. 400.

GEORGE IV 1820–1830

The death of George III on 29th January 1820 did not bring about the introduction of new gold coins for that year. Orders were issued to the Mint to continue using the old dies of George III.

At that time only Pistrucci and William Wyon were employed by the Mint as engravers. There was nothing to indicate at that time the exciting changes that would happen to the half sovereign, and indeed to other coins.

However, on 11th February 1820 a Frenchman named Jean Baptiste Merlen was added to the Mint staff of engravers; new coins were imminent, perhaps? Then an order of council, dated 5th March 1821, decreed that sovereigns and half sovereigns should be struck for that year. These coins were proclaimed current on 5th May 1821.

The first half sovereign to appear carried George IV's laureated bust by Pistrucci on its obverse. The reverse was a magnificent garnished shield, surrounded by roses, thistles and shamrocks. Alas this beautiful coin was to be in circulation only for the year of 1821. It was then withdrawn because of its likeness to the current sixpence which was being gilded and passed as a half sovereign. I fear that owing to these circumstances few of these beautiful coins will have survived; when they were recalled they would, I am sure, have been melted.

The half sovereign was re-issued in 1823 with the same obverse, but this time with a very plain and ordinary shield on the reverse, this type was to last until 1825.

A new coinage was ordered on 14th June 1825. The gold coins mentioned in this order were a £5 piece, £2 piece, sovereign and half sovereign. At this point it is necessary for me to tell you of an earlier happening; in 1823 a bust of the King in the form of a medallion was prepared by Sir Francis Chantrey which so impressed the King that he requested its use on the new coinage. Pistrucci refused to carry out this mundane task and as a result fell from favour. On 23rd June 1824 the Master of the Mint reported to the Treasury that he "thought it proper to employ Mr. Merlen to prepare the several designs and also to engrave the Dies for the reverses intended to be struck on the whole series of gold and silver coins". So as a result of these happenings the final type of half sovereign appeared with Chantrey's bust of the King, bare headed and engraved by W. Wyon; the reverse was a garnished shield engraved by J. B. Merlen from his own design. This type of half sovereign was struck and issued as currency bearing the dates 1826, 1827 and 1828. Though there is mint evidence stating that 4205 half sovereigns were struck in 1829 none have appeared bearing this date

4

and I feel these would probably have been struck from dies of the previous year.

Most of the half sovereigns of George IV can be found, and only the first, date 1821, will present real difficulty. This is quite a rare coin and a sum probably in excess of £1000 would be necessary to buy a nice specimen, if it were available. The more common dates would cost about £500 to £600 each.

Description and details (Laureate Head), Type I

Type I Obverse. The King's bust facing left, laureate, tye with loop and two ends, hair short and bare neck. B.P. in small letters below truncation standing for Benedetto Pistrucci.
Legend GEORGIUS IIII D: G: BRITANNIAR: REX F: D:
Reverse. A garnished shield, surmounted by the royal crown, bearing the Ensigns Armorial of the United Kingdom. The Hanoverian arms within an escutcheon surmounted by the royal crown in the centre of the shield. The shield surrounded by roses, thistles and shamrocks. ANNO to the left reading downwards, the date on the right reading upwards. The letters W.W.P. standing for William Wellesley Pole, then Master of the Mint, are in the respective centres of three of the shamrock leaves. The coin is struck with a reverse die axis.
Edge. Cross graining.

Description and details (Laureate Head), Type II

Type II Obverse. As Type I.
Reverse. A plain square shield, surmounted by the royal crown, bearing the Ensigns Armorial of the United Kingdom. The Hanoverian arms within an escutcheon surmounted by the royal crown in the centre of the shield. ANNO to the left reading upwards, the date on the right reading downwards. Below the shield a thistle and shamrock emerging from a rose. The coin is struck with a reverse die axis.
Edge. Cross graining.

Description and details (Bare Head)

Obverse. The King's head facing left bare. Date shown below truncation. Inscription reads GEORGIUS IV DEI GRATIA and begins and ends with a small oval flower stop.
Reverse. A garnished shield, surmounted by the royal crown, bearing the Ensigns Armorial of the United Kingdom. The Hanoverian arms within an escutcheon surmounted by the royal crown in the centre of the shield. Legend reading BRITANNIARUM REX FID: DEF: The coin is struck with a reverse die axis.
Edge. Cross graining.

LAUREATE HEAD HALF SOVEREIGNS OF GEORGE IV

NO.	DATE	VARIETIES	MINTAGE	RATING
403	1821	Type I.R. Heavily garnished shield	231,288	R2
404	1823	Type II.R. Plain square shield	224,280	S
405	1824	Type II.R. Plain square shield	591,538	N
406	1825	Type II.R. Plain square shield	761,150	N

BARE HEAD HALF SOVEREIGNS OF GEORGE IV

NO.	DATE	VARIETIES	MINTAGE	RATING
407	1826	R. Garnished shield	344,830	N
408	1827	R. ,, ,,	492,014	N
409	1828	R. ,, ,,	1,224,754	N

Plate 2

Actual size

Obverse and Reverse of 'Laureate Head' Half Sovereign No. 403.

Obverse and Reverse of 'Laureate Head' Half Sovereign No. 405.

GEORGE IV

Plate 3

Actual size

Obverse and Reverse of 'Bare Head' Half Sovereign No. 408.

WILLIAM IV 1830–1837

Though William IV succeeded his brother on 26th June 1830 no currency gold coins were issued for that year. An Order in Council, dated 22nd November 1830, did however specify that a double sovereign, sovereign and half sovereign be struck in gold. These became current by proclamation on 13th April 1831, although the double sovereign was not issued.

The first of the new sovereigns did not appear until 1834; the delay I am sure must have been worth while as the gold coins of William are, I feel, second to none. The obverse was engraved by William Wyon from a superb bust of William IV by Chantrey, the reverse a magnificently garnished shield modelled and engraved by Merlen. Both the obverse and reverse are beautifully proportioned and thus fully embellish this magnificent half sovereign of William. The overall design differs only slightly from that of the sovereign, the main difference being seen in the diminishing panels that appear in the lower garnishment on either side of the shield of both coins. On the half sovereign these panels are filled with diagonal lines giving a shaded appearance, whereas on the sovereign small round pellets are shown in this area.

Some other important facts must be mentioned concerning the 1834 half sovereign. It was in fact smaller than previous half sovereigns. The normal coin measured 19.3 mm, the new 1834 coin 17.8 mm. Though smaller in size the fineness and weight of this variety does not differ from that of the normal size half sovereigns. Finally, though a Treasury order dated 14th April 1835, requested that a reduced size half sovereign be struck, the only coins answering this description are those dated 1834.

Normal size coins appear for the years 1835, 1836 and 1837, and generally speaking they are the same as the previous variety. However, there are slight but definite changes on the reverse of this variety. The band that holds the lower garnishing together which is void on the 1834 coin this time has a bar in it, and the centre segment of this lower garnishing has an incuse line just inside the outer edge.

Finally, a third type emerges in this reign, dated 1836. This variety was for some reason struck from the sixpence die; a seemingly stupid mistake, particularly as the first variety I described, the 1834 coin, was deliberately reduced in size to avoid its being associated with the sixpence. The forger quickly reacted to this situation; he had little difficulty in gilding the sixpence. However, the 1834 half sovereign was apparently withdrawn after its first year and undoubtedly melted. Bearing in mind these circumstances it does seem strange that this third type, being struck from the sixpence die, should exist. I cannot offer any reasonable explanation as to why the sixpence die should have been used.

Really good grade half sovereigns of William IV are very scarce indeed, in fact they are seldom offered in any grade. As far as price is concerned the collector can expect to have to pay probably in excess of £600 for the least difficult coins of the reign, those dated 1835 and 1837. The other dates may cost him a four figure sum each. The rarest of the William half sovereigns is the 1836 coin, struck from the sixpence die, which is very rare and seldom seen. A specimen in around fine condition would cost about £1700 if it were available.

Description and details

Obverse. The bare head of the King facing right.
Legend GULIELMUS IIII D:G:BRITANNIAR: REX F:D:
Reverse. A garnished shield surmounted by a royal crown, bearing the Ensigns Armorial of the United Kingdom. The Hanoverian arms within an escutcheon surmounted by the royal crown in the centre of the shield. The date is shown in the field at the bottom of the right side, the word ANNO appears in a similar position on the left side. The coin is struck with a reverse die axis.
Edge. Cross graining.

HALF SOVEREIGNS OF WILLIAM IV

NO.	DATE	VARIETIES	MINTAGE	RATING
410	1834	Small size (17.8 mm.)	133,899	R
411	1835	Normal size (19.3 mm.)	772,554	S
412	1836	,, ,, ,,	146,865	R2
412A	1836	Obv. struck from sixpence die (19.4 mm.)	Not known	R5
413	1837	Normal size (19.3 mm.)	160,207	R

WILLIAM IV

Plate 4

Actual size

Obverse and Reverse of 'Small Size' Half Sovereign No. 410.

Actual size

Obverse and Reverse of Half Sovereign No. 413.

WILLIAM IV

Plate 5

Actual size

Obverse of Half Sovereign No. 412A.

VICTORIA 1837–1901

The long reign of Queen Victoria was to produce an abundance of gold coins. For those who are interested in modern coinage many varieties can be found within it, indeed one could quite happily spend a lifetime just amongst the coins of Victoria.

Queen Victoria began her reign upon the death of her uncle on 20th June 1837. An order of Council was issued on 8th June 1838 followed by a proclamation on 5th July ordering the striking of £5 pieces, sovereigns and half sovereigns, all to be of the same type as described in the order.

Patterns of a different design of £5 piece were also produced. These were the well known Una and Lion type, but they were never issued to the public. The sovereign and the half sovereign were the only gold coins to be struck for currency during Victoria's reign.

The designs for the new coinage were engraved by William Wyon obverse, and J. B. Merlen the reverse. Wyon, who was the Mint Engraver, did in fact visit Windsor Castle at Queen Victoria's request to model the Queen from life. The bust of the Queen on the first gold coins was said to be an excellent likeness.

The Type IA shield currency half sovereign of Victoria first appears bearing the date of 1838, the obverse features the lovely Wyon bust of the Queen, the reverse a garnished shield. The obverse is the same as the sovereign except that Wyon's initials W.W. do not appear on the truncation. The reverse is where the major changes have occurred. Gone are the laurel branches from either side of the shield, and in their place a lovely garnishing has been added to the shield. The shield this time contains only the arms of England, Scotland and Ireland, the escutcheon with the Hanoverian arms has been omitted. The reason for this is because the right to the Kingdom of Hanover was limited to the male line of succession.

This design of half sovereign continues until 1863, but like the sovereign the half appears with frequent variations during this period, and many can be attributed to the engraver touching up the dies. It is also known that the Mint themselves introduced minor variations just "to titillate the numismatists." (Craig, *The Mint*, p. 294).

However, within this first series there are significant variations that enable it to be categorised into two easily recognisable groups. I will refer to these groups by numbering the obverses and lettering the reverses.

Type IA shield half sovereigns dated 1838 to 1871

Obverse 1. The bust on these coins is the smallest of all Type I coins. The front ribbon on the top of the head is noticeably wider than the other ribbons. The lower truncation does not enter into the area of the legend. The date figures are normally of the small type; however, larger figures are occasionally found intermingled with the small figures. This is something that happens throughout the Type I series. The larger figures are used on a more regular basis from 1882 onwards. The reverse of this type I will call A. The details are as described earlier.

The first change in the Type IA coins appears on those dated 1859 to 1871.

Obverse 2. The bust on this obverse is slightly larger than that of obverse 1. This causes the hair to become noticeably nearer to the G in GRATIA, and the small strand of hair that came out from behind the bun has been removed. The reverse of this type is the normal kind A except for one interesting addition. A small dot is shown just above the centre of the crossed lines that divide the Ensigns Armorial. These small but definite alterations do not, I feel, spoil the beauty of Victoria's first half sovereign.

Another variation I must mention in this period is dated 1871, and the particular half sovereign of which I am able to give details of is in the British Museum collection. On this coin the bust is slightly turned causing Victoria's nose to point just above the letter T in the legend. The date figures are set slightly wider apart, and there is a die flaw running through the first A in GRATIA. The A in VICTORIA has clearly been re-entered. The reverse is similar to Type IB and that of the other variations. However, it does not have the dot on the vertical line of the cross. This particular variant is at this time extremely rare, in fact I believe it is the only known example. However, it is without doubt a currency type coin and there is enough evidence to suggest that others may well have been struck. It is, though, quite remarkable to find this date without a die number.

The Type IA half sovereigns are difficult to acquire especially in top condition as they seldom appear. The more common dates in about extremely fine condition will cost about £160 each. The 1854 coin is the rarest of this type. However, the 1848/7 overdate must be considered in the same bracket, for few overdates exist. Another very rare date is that of 1862, and these three half sovereigns could well cause an empty space in the collector's tray for a very long time. They would also cost a great deal of money.

Description and details

Obverse. Young head of Victoria to left. Hair bound with double fillet and collected into knot behind. Legend VICTORIA DEI GRATIA. Date is shown in field below truncation.

Reverse. The Ensigns Armorial within a garnished shield surmounted by a crown. A small flower stop appears in the field either side of the lower garnishing at the bottom of the coin.
Legend BRITANNIARUM REGINA FID:DEF: The coin is struck with a reverse die axis.
Edge. Cross graining.

TYPE IA. SHIELD HALF SOVEREIGNS OF VICTORIA
(LONDON MINT: NO MINT MARK)

NO.	DATE	VARIETIES	MINTAGE	RATING
414	1838	Obv. 1. Small bust. Rev. Garnished shield	273,341	R
415	1841		508,835	R
416	1842		2,223,352	N
417	1843		1,251,762	R
418	1844		1,127,007	N
419	1845		887,526	R2
420	1846		1,063,928	S
421	1847		928,636	S
422	1848		410,595	S
422A	1848/7	Obv. Overdate 8 over 7	Not known	R6
423	1849		845,112	S
424	1850		179,595	R2
425	1851		773,575	N
426	1852		1,377,671	N
427	1853		2,708,796	N
428	1854		1,125,144	R6
429	1855		1,120,362	N
430	1856		2,391,909	N
431	1857		728,223	S
432	1858		855,578	S
433	1859	Obv. 2. Slightly larger bust. Rev. Garnished shield with dot	2,203,813	N
434	1860		1,131,500	N
435	1861		1,130,867	N
436	1862		Not known	R5
437	1863		See Type IB No. 439	N
438	1871		Not known	R4

Type IB (Die Number) shield half sovereigns dated 1863 to 1880

Obverses 2, 3 and 4. It is on the Type IB half sovereigns that the next major variation can be seen. The reverse this time has a small number placed between the flower stops at the bottom of the coin. This is known as a die number, and was, I believe, introduced to give definite identification of the die itself and probably other information regarding the press and its operator.

To accommodate the new number the shield has been raised so that is actually touches the toothing at the top. On this type the obverse is the same as obverse 2 on the Type IA coins. A third obverse variation can be found on the coins of this group dated 1872 to 1877. On these coins the bust is again larger, the lower point of the truncation projects well into the legend and date area, and the front ribbon on the top of the head is still wider than the others.

A fourth obverse variation is found on the coins dated 1876 to 1880. Again the bust is slightly increased in size causing the bun to almost touch the G in GRATIA and this time the wider front ribbon on the top of the head is replaced by one that matches the others in size.

Apart from the main variations which I have just described there are two others that warrant separate mention. First, two half sovereigns dated 1871 and bearing the die number 10 were discovered by fellow collector and numismatist Ernest Faver of London. The bust on these variations appeared to have been slightly turned causing Victoria's nose to point between the letters T and O in the legend, while the whole bust is shown well out of the central position and clearly to the left. The border toothing is considerably larger creating a much coarser effect. The reverse apart from the larger toothing is the normal type, and like the British Museum variation no dot is shown on the reverse cross. The other variation is a half sovereign belonging to the Fitzwilliam Museum in Cambridge. This coin is the same as the two 1871 pieces I have just described except that it is dated 1870 and carries the die number 3.

Most of the die number half sovereigns can be acquired, and only the condition will present the collector with problems. The common dates will cost about £150 each for coins in about extremely fine condition.

Description and details

As Type IA except for die number. The coin is struck with a reverse die axis.

TYPE IB (DIE NUMBER).
SHIELD HALF SOVEREIGNS OF VICTORIA

NO.	DATE	VARIETIES	MINTAGE	RATING
439	1863	Obv. 2. Rev. Garnished shield with dot	1,571,574*	R
440	1864		1,758,490	N
441	1865		1,834,750	N
442	1866		2,058,776	N
443	1867		992,795	N
444	1869		1,861,764	N
445	1870		981,408	N
445A	1870	Obv. Bust to left. Coarse toothing	Not known	R3
446	1871		2,217,760	N
446A	1871	Obv. Bust to left. Coarse toothing	Not known	R3
447	1872	Obv. 3. Larger bust	3,235,112	N
448	1873		2,003,464	N
449	1874		1,883,872	N
450	1875		516,240	N
451	1876	Obv. 4. Bust again enlarged	2,785,187	N
452	1877		2,197,482	N
453	1878		2,081,941	N
454	1879		35,201	R
455	1880		See Type IC No. 456	N

* This mintage figure includes those of the Type IA half sovereigns of the same date.

DIE NUMBERS SO FAR KNOWN

1863   1, 2, 3, 4, 7, 9.

1864   4, 5, 8, 9, 10, 13, 14, 15, 16, 21, 22, 23, 24, 25, 27, 28, 29, 30, 31, 33, 34, 35, 36.

1865   1, 2, 5, 6, 7, 9, 10, 11, 13, 15, 18, 19, 20, 21, 22, 23, 25, 26, 27, 32, 33, 37, 38, 39, 40, 44, 45, 48, 49, 50, 52, 53, 54, 57.

1866   1, 2, 3, 4, 5, 6, 7, 9, 11, 12, 13, 15, 16, 17, 19, 21, 22, 23, 24, 26, 27, 28, 31, 32, 33, 34, 35, 36, 38.

1867   3, 4, 5, 6, 7, 8, 9, 10, 11, 12, 13, 14, 15, 18, 19, 20, 21.

1869   1, 4, 5, 6, 7, 8, 9, 10, 11, 12, 13, 16, 17, 18, 19, 20, 23, 24, 25, 26, 29.

1870   1, 3, 4, 5, 6, 33, 35, 36, 37, 38, 40, 41, 42, 43, 44, 46.

1871   1, 5, 7, 8, 9, 10, 11, 12, 13, 14, 17, 18, 26, 33, 34, 35, 38, 41, 47, 50, 55, 56, 57, 58, 60, 61, 62, 63, 64, 65, 67, 69, 81, 92.

1872   17, 29, 30, 34, 37, 40, 41, 42, 43, 49, 50, 57, 62, 70, 75, 79, 85, 86, 94, 99, 100, 102, 104, 105, 106, 110, 112, 119, 120, 126, 138, 141, 142, 143, 151, 154, 165, 173, 186, 192, 195, 196, 198, 200, 202, 203, 212, 214, 223, 245, 251, 255, 274, 293, 296, 297, 320, 331, 335, 338, 341, 346, 349, 350, 353, 363, 369, 380, 391.

1873   3, 15, 20, 31, 32, 49, 56, 65, 89, 94, 99, 103, 147, 158, 171, 184, 197, 201, 205, 220, 226, 233, 238, 245, 247, 257, 258, 263, 268, 269, 275, 279, 280, 283, 290, 295, 296, 299, 300, 308, 315, 319, 334, 335, 394, 406, 407, 414.

1874   1, 2, 4, 8, 12, 13, 14, 15, 17, 19, 21, 23, 24, 25, 26, 31, 33, 38, 41, 44, 45, 47, 50, 54, 66, 68, 74, 212, 338, 341, 342.

1875   5, 6, 8, 12, 15, 17, 22, 23, 24, 26, 47, 53, 72, 280.

1876   2, 3, 6, 9, 10, 13, 15, 17, 20, 21, 22, 25, 27, 29, 34, 37, 41, 43, 44, 45, 47, 49, 51, 52, 55, 57, 58, 62, 63, 65, 69, 71, 72, 73, 74, 79, 81, 83, 84, 85, 86, 87, 88, 89, 98, 101.

1877   3, 11, 16, 21, 22, 25, 28, 29, 31, 32, 33, 37, 39, 43, 46, 47, 49, 51, 53, 54, 55, 56, 57, 58, 61, 62, 63, 64, 65, 66, 71, 73, 80, 85, 94, 97, 100, 103, 105, 108, 109, 110, 114, 115, 120, 124, 125, 126, 127, 130, 134, 135, 136, 137, 139, 143, 147, 150, 151, 154, 155, 160, 245.

1878   2, 4, 8, 9, 10, 11, 13, 14, 15, 17, 20, 21, 24, 25, 28, 29, 32, 34, 35, 36, 37, 38, 40, 45, 46, 48, 53, 56, 59, 62, 65, 66, 69, 71, 72, 73, 76, 78, 81, 92, 97, 98, 100, 101, 105, 108, 113, 130, 149, 156, 158, 162, 167, 197.

1879   57, 88, 89, 95, 112, 119, 180.

1880   3, 75, 78, 103, 104, 108, 110, 111, 114, 115, 118, 119, 121, 123, 124, 125, 129, 131.

Type IC Shield half sovereigns dated 1880 to 1885

Obverse 5. This variety does not carry a die number. The obverse is shown in low relief and also has the largest bust of all Type I coins, and because of this part of the bun is clearly inside the legend area. The lower truncation point is in a similar position and also touches the date. The thickening of the rim and toothing is also very evident, and this coupled with the large bust gives an overall cramped impression. The reverse is similar to the die number variety; the shield retains its high position and the cross on the top of the crown actually encroaches under the toothing at the top. Because of the rim thickening, the legend is very close to the toothing, this also affects the flower stops at the bottom though they have in fact been slightly lowered.

Most of the Type IC coins are not too difficult to find except in really top grade. The common dates in about extremely fine condition will cost about £140 each. The key coin of this type is the 1885 over 3. This very rare overdate will not be easy to acquire. It will certainly cost a great deal of money when the collector is lucky enough to find it.

Description and details

As Type IA. The coin is struck with a reverse die axis.

TYPE IC. SHIELD HALF SOVEREIGNS OF VICTORIA (NO DIE NUMBER) HEAD IN LOW RELIEF

NO.	DATE	VARIETIES	MINTAGE	RATING
456	1880	Obv. 5. Largest bust	1,009,049*	R
457	1883		2,807,411	C
458	1884		1,121,600	N
459	1885		4,533,605	C
459A	1885/3	Obv. Overdate 5 over 3	Not known	R5

* This mintage figure includes those of the Type IB half sovereigns of the same date.

Types ID and IE are the final half sovereigns to bear the young head design. They were struck at the Sydney and Melbourne mints of Australia. In 1851 gold was discovered in Australia, because of this heavy demands were made on the coinage of the colonies. Such heavy demands could not be met, and a petition by the Council of New South Wales was addressed to Her Majesty on 19th December 1851 asking that a branch of the Royal Mint be set up in Sydney.

An order of Council dated 19th August 1853 authorised the Sydney Mint, and it opened on 14th May 1855. A similar branch was opened in Melbourne on 12th June 1872. The Perth Mint in Western Australia did not open until 20th June 1899.

An act was passed in 1863 stating that Queen Victoria had by proclamation established the Sydney branch mint for making gold coins. They were to be the same as those issued by the Royal Mint in London. It would be lawful for the Queen by Proclamation, and with the advice of her Privy Council, to declare that after a given date in the Proclamation gold coins made at the branch mint of designs approved by Her Majesty, should be the same fineness and weight as those struck at the Royal Mint, London. They would then be legal tender within the United Kingdom of Britain and Ireland. In 1866 the Colonial Branch Mint Act was passed which gave general power to the Queen by Proclamation, and so because of the two Acts coins struck at the branch mints would be legal tender.

The first coins struck at the branch mints were not accepted as currency outside New South Wales. This was because they were not struck bearing a design by the Royal Mint, nor of course were they approved by Her Majesty. Imperial design half sovereigns were first struck at the Sydney Mint in 1871, and the Melbourne Mint in 1873. The dies for these coins were sunk, complete with mint mark and date, at the Royal Mint in London, and were transported to Australia by ship.

Bearing in mind these known facts, it is not surprising to find that the coins are of the same design as those from the Royal Mint in London of the corresponding years. The only major difference is that the mint marks S or M, for Sydney or Melbourne, appear on the reverse of the coin below the shield. However, the Sydney Mint has one most interesting variety, dated 1872. This half sovereign is quite different from other Sydney issues. The bust of Victoria has been slightly turned causing the nose to point towards the letter T in the legend. Normally the nose points towards the letter O. The legend itself is also slightly re-arranged. All half sovereigns of the Sydney Mint of 1872 are of this type.

The collector will not find it easy to acquire the half sovereigns of Sydney or Melbourne. Both these branch mints have produced some very rare coins, so rest assured that on the few occasions they appear they will be very costly, especially if they are top grade coins. At a recent auction of Spink Auctions (Australia) Pty Ltd., I noted that an 1887 Type IE Melbourne half sovereign was offered. It was described as nearly uncirculated and it fetched £3550! However the more common coins in around extremely fine condition will cost about £200 each.

Description and details

As Type IA except that the mint mark, as S or M, appears below the lower garnishing on the reverse.

TYPE ID. SHIELD HALF SOVEREIGNS OF VICTORIA
(SYDNEY MINT: MINT MARK S)

NO.	DATE	VARIETIES	MINTAGE	RATING
460	1871	Obv. 2 Rev. Garnished shield with dot	Not known	S
461	1872*	Obv. Victoria's nose points to T in legend	356,000	N
462	1875		Not known	N
463	1879		94,000	S
464	1880		80,000	S
465	1881		62,000	R2
466	1882		52,000	R2
467	1883		220,000	N
468	1886		82,000	S
469	1887		134,000	N

* This year only.

TYPE IE. SHIELD HALF SOVEREIGNS OF VICTORIA
(MELBOURNE MINT: MINT MARK M)

NO.	DATE	VARIETIES	MINTAGE	RATING
470	1873		165,034	N
471	1877		80,016	S
472	1881		42,009	R
473	1882		107,522	S
474	1884		48,009	R
475	1885		11,003	R5
476	1886		38,008	R2
477	1887		64,013	R2

JUBILEE half sovereigns dated 1887 to 1893

In 1887 the fiftieth anniversary of the Queen's accession was marked by a new coinage. The Queen indicated that she was extremely pleased with a portrait medallion by Mr. J. E. Boehm, R.A. which had been modelled from life. The Queen herself requested that this should replace the Wyon effigy which had been in use up to that time. The effigy for the new coinage was fashioned in plaster, and from this

21

model copies were made in metal taken by electro-deposition; these were then reduced by machinery to the required sizes for the different dies.

The first half sovereign to feature the new Boehm bust is dated 1887. It shows the Queen facing left wearing a small crown, veiled and with ribbon and star of the Garter and the Victoria and Albert Order. The legend inside the border and Boehm's initials are at the bottom of the bust. The reverse again has the garnished shield but the small flower stops at the bottom have been omitted to make way for the date. The legend remains the same as before.

There are a number of variations which I will explain in the best way possible. During the past few months I have examined upwards of 150 Jubilee half sovereigns, including some 30 coins of the branch mints. In spite of this, I cannot with any confidence, put into definite order the variations I have noted on these coins. However, they are genuine and it is important that they are noted. The variations mainly concern the obverse of the Jubilee half sovereigns, and my attention was first drawn to this by Mr. E. G. V. Newman's article which appeared in the *The Numismatic Circular* of December 1977. He reported that two half sovereigns though of the same date were from different dies. One carried the initials of the designer J.E.B. (Joseph Edgar Boehm), but the other coin did not. However, they were both genuine. The variations I have seen are J.E.B. in large letters but with the bottom loop of the J missing; J.E.B. in large letters but with perfect J; J.E.B. in smaller letters set fairly close together, and J.E.B. again in small letters but widely spaced. Because of the irregular way that these variations appear throughout this type I cannot place them in any logical order. Many more examples will need to be examined, but even then I feel a definite order may not emerge.

There are also differences that appear on the reverse of the Jubilee half sovereign. The date figures on the first issue are shown fairly close together thus causing the shield to be positioned quite high on the coin, in fact the topmost point of the crown encroaches well into the toothing. Another point that I have noticed on this first issue is that the last colon is shown slanting inwards (D E F.) This seems only to occur on the coins dated 1887. The other reverse variation shows the shield slightly lowered causing the space in the centre of the date to become much wider as the figures are parted to allow room for the lower garnishing. Again I am unable to establish a definite order for the two reverses.

As well as at the London Mint the half sovereign was struck at the branch mints of Melbourne and Sydney. Generally speaking the collector will be able to acquire all of the London Mint dates without too much difficulty, for they frequently appear in really nice condition. The common dates should cost about £110 each. However, the branch mints will not be so easy, and an extremely fine specimen of the more common dates will cost about £180.

Description and details

Obverse. The bust of the Queen facing left wearing a small crown, veiled and with ribbon and Star of the Garter and the Victoria and Albert Order. Boehm's initials J.E.B. are shown raised at the bottom rear of the bust.*
Legend VICTORIA DEI GRATIA.
Reverse. The Ensigns Armorial within a garnished shield and surmounted by an imperial crown.
Legend BRITANNIARUM REGINA FID:DEF. · The date is shown below the shield.
Edge. Cross graining.
* See notes on J.E.B. variations on page 22.

JUBILEE HALF SOVEREIGNS OF VICTORIA
(LONDON MINT: NO MINT MARK)

NO.	DATE	VARIETIES	MINTAGE	RATING
478	1887		841,200	N
479	1890		2,243,200	C
480	1891		1,079,286	N
481	1892		13,680,486	C
482	1893		4,426,625	N

Description and details (Melbourne and Sydney)

As for the London Mint except that the mint mark, an M or S, appears below the lower garnishing on the reverse.

JUBILEE HALF SOVEREIGNS OF VICTORIA
(MELBOURNE MINT: MINT MARK M)

NO.	DATE	VARIETIES	MINTAGE	RATING
483	1887		Not known	S
484	1893		110,024	S

JUBILEE HALF SOVEREIGNS OF VICTORIA
(SYDNEY MINT: MINT MARK S)

NO.	DATE	VARIETIES	MINTAGE	RATING
485	1887		Not known	N
486	1889		64,000	S
487	1891		154,000	N

OLD HEAD half sovereigns dated 1893 to 1901

February 1891 marked the beginning of the final change in Victoria's coinage. At the request of the Chancellor of the Exchequer a committee met to consider and report the designs for coinage. Designs had been submitted by Mr. H. H. Armstead, R.A., Mr. C. B. Birch, A.R.A., Mr. T. Brock, R.A., Mr. E. O. Ford, A.R.A. and Mr. W. H. Thorneycroft, R.A., all of whom were leading sculptors of the day. A design was also submitted by Mr. E. J. Poynter, R.A. who was a painter. Following the recommendation of this committee the Queen chose an effigy by Thomas Brock, and this was to be used on the obverse of all future gold and silver coins.

The new Brock bust appeared on the half sovereign for the first time dated 1893. The Queen is seen in much older form, veiled and draped, the legend including for the first time IND.IMP. (Empress of India). These letters were added because of the Proclamation of 1876 concerning provisions of Royal Titles.

The reverse of the half sovereign this time shows a complete change, and what a change it is! Benedetto Pistrucci's legendary design of St. George slaying the dragon appears for the first time on the half sovereign. Pistrucci's initials B.P. do not appear on this type.

The half sovereigns for this final period of Victoria's reign were struck at the London Mint, Melbourne Mint, Sydney Mint and for the first time at the Perth Mint. Those from the London Mint will not present the collector with any problems, and he should acquire all dates in good grade at about £100 each. Halves from the branch mints will not be so easy, far fewer were struck and as a result they are not often offered. When the more common dates appear they will probably cost about £160 each for a nice specimen.

It is worth mentioning at this point the 1893 Melbourne Mint half sovereign; many numismatists have raised doubts as to whether it exists. Well, I can definitely confirm that the coin does exist in currency form the Royal Australian Mint have confirmed to me that they have a currency piece of this date in their coin museum. However, it must be said that this particular date is one of the rarest throughout the Victorian period. Few collections will have an example of it.

Description and details

Obverse. The bust of the Queen facing left, crowned, veiled and draped, wearing ribbon and Star of the Garter. The small letters T.B. appear below the bust.
Legend
VICTORIA·DEI·GRA·BRITT·REGINA·FID·DEF·IND·IMP·
Reverse. St. George mounted with streamer flowing from helmet, slaying the dragon with sword. The date is shown below the exergue line.
Edge. Cross graining.

The branch mint coins are the same except that the mint mark, an M, P or S, is shown in the centre of the exergue line on the reverse.

OLD HEAD HALF SOVEREIGNS OF VICTORIA
(LONDON MINT: NO MINT MARK)

NO.	DATE	VARIETIES	MINTAGE	RATING
488	1893		Not known	C
489	1894		3,794,591	C
490	1895		2,869,183	C
491	1896		2,946,605	C
492	1897		3,568,156	C
493	1898		2,868,527	C
494	1899		3,361,881	C
495	1900		4,307,372	C
496	1901		2,037,664	C

OLD HEAD HALF SOVEREIGNS OF VICTORIA
(MELBOURNE MINT: MINT MARK M)

NO.	DATE	VARIETIES	MINTAGE	RATING
497	1893		Not known	R6
498	1896		218,946	N
499	1899		97,221	S
500	1900		112,920	N

OLD HEAD HALF SOVEREIGNS OF VICTORIA
(PERTH MINT: MINT MARK P)

NO.	DATE	VARIETIES	MINTAGE	RATING
501	1900		119,376	S

OLD HEAD HALF SOVEREIGNS OF VICTORIA
(SYDNEY MINT: MINT MARK S)

NO.	DATE	VARIETIES	MINTAGE	RATING
502	1893		250,000	N
503	1897		Not known	N
504	1900		260,000	N

Plate 6

Actual size

Obverse and Reverse of Type IA (Obv. 1) Shield Half Sovereign No. 427.

Obverse and Reverse of Type IA (Obv. 2) Shield Half Sovereign No. 435.

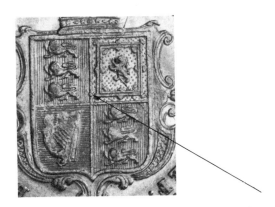

'The dot' found on the Reverse of Type IA Half Sovereigns
1859 to 1871.

Plate 7

Obverse and Reverse of Type IB (Die No.) Shield Half Sovereign
No. 454.

Obverse and Reverse of Type IC (Obv. 5) Shield Half Sovereign
No. 459.

VICTORIA

Plate 8

Obverse and Reverse of Type ID Sydney Mint Shield Half Sovereign
No. 469.

Obverse and Reverse of Type IE Melbourne Mint Shield Half
Sovereign No. 476.

Plate 9

Obverse and Reverse of Type IA (Variant) Shield Half Sovereign
No. 438.

Obverse and Reverse of Type IB (Variant) Shield Half Sovereign
No. 445A.

Plate 10

Obverse and Reverse of Type IB (Variant) Shield Half Sovereign
No. 446A.

The Scanning Electron Microscope

Before moving to the next group of photographs it is necessary for me to explain a little about them; they are in fact rather special and were taken by the camera of a Scanning Electron Microscope. A few months ago I was able to examine a sovereign overdate on this microscope, and it was in fact the first time that this wonderful piece of modern technology had been used for this purpose. It enabled positive identification to be made. The Scanning Microscope uses a very fine beam of electrons to scan the surface of the sample, and the electrons reflected from the sample can be detected and transformed into a television image on the screen of the microscope. Surface details are imaged as regions of different contrast and can then be photographed for reference.

I must say at this point how indebted I am to Dr. R. S. Paden of the Cambridge Scanning Co. Ltd. Dr. Paden who very kindly allowed me the facility of their Scanning Microscope, and also willingly gave much valuable time to assist in the examination of the new half sovereign overdate 1848/7. This is in fact the first overdate to be recorded from the Type IA series. There cannot be any doubt that the Scanning Microscope has a place in the world of the numismatist. It enables the most minute details to be examined and seen as never before.

The photograph with the black dividing line between the two figures is a stereo pair picture, and it is best viewed through a stereo viewer. The stereo imaging technique enables changes in height to be readily visualised by taking two separate images of the sample from different angles of tilt, and this technique aids the interpretation of the sample height changes and the details observed in the normal microscope images. The other photographs showing the date in full and of single figures are the normal type. But again they reveal much detail, especially the picture showing the figure at an angle and side on.

Plate 11

Obverse and Reverse of Type IA (Overdate) Shield Half Sovereign
No. 422A.

Photographs taken on the Scanning Electron Microscope.

Full Date of Type IA Shield Half Sovereign No. 422A.

Plate 12

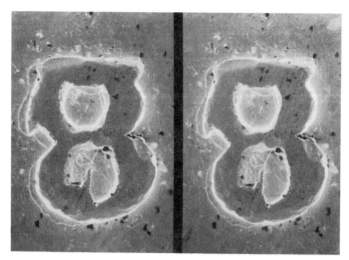

Stereo Pair Picture of 8. Type IA Shield Half Sovereign No. 422A.

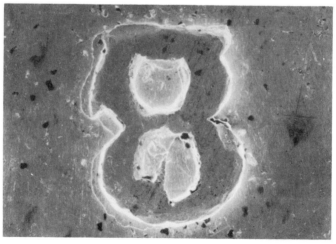

Normal photograph of 8. Type IA Shield Half Sovereign No. 422A.

VICTORIA

Plate 13

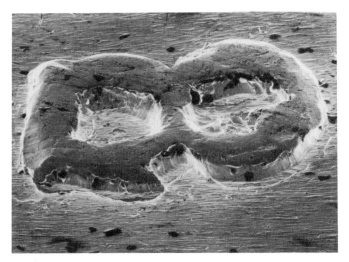

Angle and Side View of 8. Type IA Shield Half Sovereign No. 422A.

Actual size

Obverse and Reverse of Jubilee Half Sovereign No. 478.

Plate 14

Obverse and Reverse of Jubilee (Melbourne) Half Sovereign No. 483.

Obverse and Reverse of Jubilee (Sydney) Half Sovereign No. 485.

Plate 15

Imperfect J large type.   Normal large J.E.B.

Small J.E.B.   Small wide spaced J.E.B.

Plate 16

No J.E.B.

Higher shield. Figures close together.

Lower shield. Figures wider spaced.

Plate 17

Actual size

Obverse and Reverse of Old Head Half Sovereign No. 495.

Reverse of Old Head
(Melbourne)
Half Sovereign No. 498.

Reverse of Old Head (Perth)
Half Sovereign No. 501.

Plate 18

Reverse of Old Head (Sydney)
Half Sovereign No. 504.

EDWARD VII 1901–1910

Though Queen Victoria died in January 1901 no new coins were struck for that year, and all that were struck for the remainder of the year still bore Victoria's effigy.

The first issue of coins for Edward VII were struck in 1902. They were in fact authorised by Royal Proclamation on 10th December 1901.

The obverse design for the new half sovereign was designed and engraved by G. W. De Saulles, while the reverse was once again Pistrucci's St. George and the Dragon. However, although this reverse is used throughout the reign a change in design occurs in 1904.

Beginning in 1902 and continuing until 1904 we have the normal type of St. George reverse which I will call Reverse A. On this reverse the image of St. George slaying the dragon is seen with a clear space all round it, especially behind the rear of the cloak and also in front of the dragon's lower front foot. The exergue line stops well short of the border on both sides thus leaving a clear space at these points, and is also quite thick in appearance. The two reins which come from the underside of the horse's head quickly merge into one. Pistrucci's initials B.P. do not appear on this variety.

Reverse B is found on the half sovereigns dated 1904 to 1910. This time the image of St. George slaying the dragon has been noticeably changed. Overall it is slightly larger and because of this enlargement both the rear of the cloak and the lower front foot of the dragon are nearer to the border of the coin. The exergue line also extends on both ends much closer to the border and is also thinner. The folds in the cloak are slightly re-arranged, and this time the reins which come from under the horse's head do not merge into one, they continue as a pair right up to the horse's chest. The dragon's wings have been re-designed, and the one nearer to the head is increased in size causing it to touch the dragon's neck. St. George carries his sword at a slightly lower angle. Pistrucci's initials B.P. are this time shown to the right of the date below the exergue line.

These reverses are also found on the half sovereigns struck at the branch mints. Half sovereigns dated 1904 from the London and Perth mints can be found with either reverse.

So in all, the half sovereigns of Edward were struck at the London mint and at the branch mints of Melbourne, Perth and Sydney. The branch mint of Ottawa, though striking sovereigns of this reign, did not strike any half sovereigns.

Generally speaking the collector will find it relatively easy to put together the Edward series of half sovereigns, only the Perth mint will

41

be difficult. None of the three Perth coins will be easy to find, especially the first, dated 1904, which is a very rare date and very seldom appears. Even a low grade specimen of this date would be welcome in many collections. The common coins of this reign in about extremely fine condition can be bought for about £70 each.

Description and details

Obverse. The bare head of the King facing right. The small letters De S (for De Saulles) below the truncation in relief.
Legend EDWARDVS VII D:G:BRITT:OMN:REX F:D:IND:IMP:
Reverse. St. George mounted with streamer flowing from helmet, slaying the dragon with sword. Date is shown below the exergue line with the small letters B.P. to the right in relief.*
Edge. Cross graining.
* See notes on variations on page 41.

EDWARD VII HALF SOVEREIGNS
(LONDON MINT: NO MINT MARK)

NO.	DATE	VARIETIES	MINTAGE	RATING
505	1902	Rev. A No B.P.	4,244,457	C
506	1903		2,522,057	C
507	1904	Rev. A and Rev. B with B.P.	1,717,440	N
508	1905	Rev. B. with B.P.	3,023,993	C
509	1906		4,245,437	C
510	1907		4,233,421	C
511	1908		3,996,992	C
512	1909		4,010,715	C
513	1910		5,023,881	C

Description and details

The branch mint issues are the same as those from the London Mint except that the mint mark, an M, P or S, is shown in the centre of the exergue line on the reverse.

EDWARD VII HALF SOVEREIGNS
(MELBOURNE MINT: MINT MARK M)

NO.	DATE	VARIETIES	MINTAGE	RATING
514	1906	Rev. B with B.P.	82,042	S
515	1907		405,034	N
516	1908		inc. in No. 515	N
517	1909		186,094	S

EDWARD VII HALF SOVEREIGNS
(PERTH MINT: MINT MARK P)

NO.	DATE	VARIETIES	MINTAGE	RATING
518	1904	Rev. A and Rev. B	60,030	R
519	1908	Rev. B	24,668	R
520	1909		44,022	S

EDWARD VII HALF SOVEREIGNS
(SYDNEY MINT: MINT MARK S)

NO.	DATE	VARIETIES	MINTAGE	RATING
521	1902	Rev. A	84,000	S
522	1903		231,000	N
523	1906	Rev. B	308,000	N
524	1908		538,000	C
525	1910		474,000	C

Plate 19

Obverse and Reverse of London Mint Half Sovereign No. 505.

Reverse of (Melbourne)   Reverse of (Perth)
Half Sovereign No. 516.   Half Sovereign No. 520.

EDWARD VII

Plate 20

Reverse of (Sydney)
Half Sovereign No. 525.

Plate 21

Reverse A.

Reverse B.

The Two Reverses of Edward VII Half Sovereigns.

GEORGE V 1910–1936

The reign of George V began in 1910 and during the reign several million gold coins were struck, but alas owing to the Great War of 1914–18 few were to be used as currency.

Bertram Mackennal, A.R.A., a well-known Australian sculptor, was given the task of preparing a model for the proposed new coinage. Mackennal who came from Melbourne had studied art in France and very quickly gained public recognition. He was chosen to carve statues of Queen Victoria for Australia, Lahore and England, and also designed the winner's medals for the 1908 Olympic Games which were held in London.

Mackennal's work on the new coinage began with a plaster model taken from a photograph of the King. For the final work on the new bust he was granted a special sitting by the King, and from the completed model master punches of actual coinage size were cut by a reducing machine.

The new gold coinage consisted of a £5 piece, £2 piece, sovereign and half sovereign; however, only the last two were issued as currency. The new half sovereign was first struck bearing the date of 1911. The obverse features the King bare headed facing left and the reverse is once again Pistrucci's St. George and Dragon. They were struck at the Royal Mint until 1915. When the Great War broke out in 1914 this tragic and sad event brought about the end of our gold coinage. The Government in order to preserve the gold reserve intact, apart from that paid to neutral countries for the purchase of materials, issued new Treasury notes of £1 and 10s. Sadly these took the place of the sovereign and half sovereign.

Though no more currency half sovereigns were struck at the Royal Mint after 1915, some of the branch mints continued to strike them along with other gold coins. During this reign gold coins were struck at the branch mints of Ottawa, Melbourne, Perth, Sydney and at the new mints of Bombay and Pretoria. The Bombay Mint of India opened in 1918 and struck coins for that year and 1919. The Pretoria Mint of South Africa opened in 1922. Half sovereigns were struck at all the branch mints excepting the Bombay Mint and the Ottawa Mint of Canada. They are of the same type as those from the Royal Mint except that they display a small letter indicating at which mint they were struck in the centre of the exergue line on the reverse of the coin.

None of the Royal Mint coins are difficult to obtain and it should not be a problem for the collector to find any of the dates in really nice condition, costing about £55 per coin. The branch mint coins will present some difficulty and here the collector may well have to be patient. Most will eventually turn up at probably around £75 per coin. The 1918 half sovereign from the Perth Mint is the rarest from this reign and it may well be a long time before the collector can add this one to his collection, and it will undoubtedly cost him a large sum. I noted that an E.F. specimen fetched £410 at a recent auction and I feel this buyer was very lucky as he could well have had to pay around £600. At an auction one can sometimes strike lucky!

Description and details

Obverse. The bare head of the King facing left. The small letters B.M. standing for Bertram Mackennal are shown in relief on the lower truncation towards the rear.
Legend GEORGIVS V D.G.BRITT:OMN:REX F.D.IND:IMP:
Reverse. St. George mounted with streamer flowing from helmet, slaying the dragon with a sword. Date is shown below the exergue line with the small letters B.P. to the right in relief.
Edge. Cross graining.

GEORGE V HALF SOVEREIGNS
(LONDON MINT: NO MINT MARK)

NO.	DATE	VARIETIES	MINTAGE	RATING
526	1911		6,104,106	C
527	1912		6,224,316	C
528	1913		6,094,290	C
529	1914		7,251,124	C
530	1915		2,042,747	N

Description and details

The branch mint issues are the same as those from the London Mint except that the mint mark, an M, P, S or S.A., is shown in the centre of the exergue line on the reverse.

GEORGE V HALF SOVEREIGNS
(MELBOURNE MINT: MINT MARK M)

NO.	DATE	VARIETIES	MINTAGE	RATING
531	1915		125,664	N

GEORGE V HALF SOVEREIGNS
(PERTH MINT: MINT MARK P)

NO.	DATE	VARIETIES	MINTAGE	RATING
532	1911		130,373	N
533	1915		136,219	N
534	1918		Not known	R
535	1919	Not circulated		
536	1920	,, ,,		

GEORGE V HALF SOVEREIGNS
(SYDNEY MINT: MINT MARK S)

NO.	DATE	VARIETIES	MINTAGE	RATING
537	1911		252,000	N
538	1912		278,000	N
539	1914		322,000	N
540	1915		892,000	C
541	1916		448,000	C

GEORGE V HALF SOVEREIGNS
(PRETORIA MINT SOUTH AFRICA: MINT MARK SA)

NO.	DATE	VARIETIES	MINTAGE	RATING
542	1925		946,615	C
543	1926		806,540	C

GEORGE V

Plate 22

Actual size

Obverse and Reverse of London Mint Half Sovereign No. 527.

Reverse of (Melbourne)
Half Sovereign No. 531.

Reverse of (Perth)
Half Sovereign No. 532.

Plate 23

Reverse of (Sydney)
Half Sovereign No. 541.

Reverse of (Pretoria)
Half Sovereign No. 542.

CONCLUSION

I am sure that by now you will see just how attractive the half sovereign can be. It is a series that has an abundance of interest and beauty, and there are many real gems within it. I believe this is the first time it has been given a book to itself; well, that was long overdue.

I have tried to set out the series in correct order and with all the known fact relating to it. However, I must say that we still have much to learn about the half sovereign and this publication will undoubtedly help in this respect. I am sure some of you will uncover a little more of the past relating to the half sovereign, and if so I will always be pleased to hear from you.

It is a pity that "The Gold Half Sovereign" has to conclude at George V. There were no currency half sovereigns issued during the reign of George VI or our present Queen Elizabeth II. To me, and I am sure to many collectors of gold, this is a sorry omission. Perhaps one day we shall see a currency half sovereign that carries the bust of Queen Elizabeth II.

BIBLIOGRAPHY

Sir Geoffrey Duveen and H. G. Stride	The History of the Gold Sovereign
R. L. Kenyon	The Gold Coins of England
J. J. Cullimore Allen	Sovereigns of the British Empire
B. A. Seaby Ltd.	Seaby Coin & Medal Bulletin
Spink & Son Ltd.	The Numismatic Circular
Epic Publishing Ltd. U.K.	Coin & Medal News
Numismatic Publishing Co.	Coin Monthly
Capt. K. J. Douglas Morris, R.N.	Distinguished Collection of English Gold Coins 1700–1900 (Sotheby's Sale Catalogue Nov. 1974)
Sir John Craig, K.C.V.O., C.B., LL.D.	The Mint
M. A. Marsh	The Gold Sovereign

NOTES